About the Author

Shirley Lopez, well known writer has written in many different genre's.

I feel that writing about animals would be very beneficial to help preserve the animals on earth that are about to become distinct.

It is also a way to introduce animals to those who are not familiar with how they function amongst mankind. They are our pets and creatures of the wild. We as humans should strive to protect animals and love them.

Contents:

The Owl

The **"Wise Old Owl"** sets in the tree, watching and waiting to see what he can see.

He says **"who"** when a question is ask. And when things go wrong he says "who" me.

But his head goes around and round so he can see everything in the world that will be.

Things don't always come out right but the **"Wise Old Owl"** knows best just says **"who"**

When we are wrong and when we are right the **"Wise Old Owl"** just goes **"who"** me?

The Owl comes in many
different species and
usually lives in the forest.
He is beautiful bird with
one word.

WHO

There are approximately 200
species of owls. They are
nocturnal birds meaning they

do their hunting etc. in the night.

Known well for their upright stance. The owl is one of the larger birds with large very broad head. The owl has binocular vision and binaural hearing, the bird has very sharp talons that helps when they are hunting.

The feathers help them to have a silent flight. The exception in the owl family is the gregarious burrowing owl.

The owl hunts mostly small mammals, insects, and other birds. But they prefer to hunt fish.

The owl is in all regions of the earth except the Antarctica and some very remote islands.

Mr. Owl is divided into two families. The typical owl family and the barn owl. Referred to as the Strigidae (true) and Strigidae (barn-owl) family.

Owls hunt mostly small mammals, insects, and other birds, although a few species specialize in . We think of the owl as the little creature who sets in the tree's in the forest or woods.

Owl Legends

The Native American Indian tribes believe the owl is a symbol of death. When you hear an owl hoot that means you will be unlucky.

The Indians have made them a part of many different bogey man stories. Used to help keep the children in at night or not to cry too much.

Owls are believed to be associated with ghosts. Some tribes believe that the owl can carry messages beyond the grave or carry supernatural warnings to people who have broken tribal taboos.

The Aztec and Mayan Indians of Mexico used the owl in their religions as messengers.
Not all owls are considered as death warnings. In other tribes they have a variety of meanings.

Myths and Folklore

Who

The Greek goddess of wisdom is Athena and she adopted her owl as a companion. She wanted the owl because he is known to be nocturnal. Her owl is found in great numbers inside of places like Acropolis.

Many coins amongst the Greeks are minted with the face of the owl.

The Hopi Native American Indian holds the burrowing owl as a very sacred bird. The Hopi called this owl Ko'Ko. He was the protector of the underworld and all things that grew on earth. This owl took of seeds and plants.

The Inuit people of Alaska legend is about the Snowy Owl.

The Inuit people of Alaska have a legend about <u>the Snowy Owl</u>, in which Owl and Raven are making each other new clothes. Raven made Owl a pretty dress of black and white feathers. Owl decided to make Raven a lovely white dress to wear.

However, when Owl asked Raven to allow her to fit the dress, Raven was so excited that she couldn't hold still. In fact, she jumped around so much that Owl got fed up and threw a pot of lamp oil at Raven. The lamp oil soaked through the white dress, and so Raven has been black ever since.

African Superstitions

In many African countries, the owl is associated with sorcery and baneful magic. A large owl hanging around a house is believed to indicate that a **powerful shaman** lives within.

Many people also believe
that the owl carries
messages back and forth
between the shaman
and the spirit world.

In some places, nailing an
owl to the door of a house
was considered a way to
keep evil at bay.

The tradition began in
ancient Rome, after owls
foretold the deaths of
Julius Caesar and several
other Emperors. The
custom persisted in some
areas, including Great
Britain, up through the
eighteenth century, where

an owl nailed to a barn
door protected the
livestock within from fire or
lightning.

In England it was believed
that if you walked around a
tree that an owl was
perched in, it would follow
you with its eyes, around
and around until it wrung
its own neck."

The owl was known as a
harbinger of bad tidings
and **doom** throughout
Europe, and put in
appearances as a symbol
of death and destruction in
a number of popular plays

and poems. For instance,
Sir Walter Scott wrote in _The
Legend of Montrose_:

_Birds of omen dark and
foul,
Night-crow, raven, bat,
and owl,
Leave the sick man to his
dream --
All night long he heard
your scream._

Shakespeare wrote of the
owl's premonition of death in
Macbeth and Julius Caesar.

The Little Owl

The people who live in the Appalachian area heritage is traced back to the Scottish Highlands.

These folks are associated with the cailleach and English villages that were homes of the original settlers live.

Mountain Superstitions

The fact is that because most of the people who live in the mountains have superstitions that surround the owl that relates to death.

When the owl hoots late at night that means someone will be dead by morning light.

When the owl leaves his perch during the day to circle about it means bad news will soon enter the house.

Many folks have the belief that the owl leaves his tree to eat the souls of those who are wicked when they die. Many

different people all around the
world have beliefs about the
owl. Most of those relate to
death or bad news.

Color Your Owl

The Dog

The shoes got chewed, theirs
poop on the floor, dog gone,
it's the dog.

The neighbor got mad as
hatter, the boys tore their
pants, dog-gone it's the dog.

The house got wrecked, oh
heck, the mail man won't come
to the door any more, dog
gone it's the dog.

Night time come kids to bed,
look who is sleeping at their
head. Dog-gone it's the dog.

Vacation time is coming near, and some want him so very near. Others say oh no not Rex, but you know who wins dog-gone it's the dog

Time to take a walk

Puppies

Bea-Gee My Dog

True Family Member

The dog is the true family
member that can get by with
more things than most kids.
For centuries people have
loved the dog keep him in their
home as pets.

Most dogs have their own bed
along with being fed and
water. Many are even

pampered with special baths
and grooming. We love them
dear and often it is said that if
they grow sick or found dead
we grieve their loss just like a
person. But dog-gone he is
just the dog.

Dog lovers have always felt
that the dog is very smart and
knows what you are saying. If
you don't believe it just ask the
dog.

History of the Dog

The archaeological society
declared that the dog
dates to more than 10,000

years. Time has proven
that man has loved the
dog most all his life.

Remains of the dog have
been found in Denmark
and West Germany dating
back centuries.

Very likely, the canine is
the result of a mixing of
genes from the many
different types of canids,
which is the family of
which the dog is a
member.

Other members include
wolves,
coyotes, jackals, dingoes and

foxes, all of which can
interbreed.   There are over
30
different species of
canids. They exist
everywhere - from the jungles
of South America to
the glaciers of Arctic Canada

Not only do dogs share
physical similarities between
the skeletal structure of other
canids, many behavioral and
instinctive traits we see
demonstrated by our
domesticated dogs are
typical of the pack hierarchy
of canids. Canids are noted
for their intelligence,

strength and adaptability. .

Stone-aged people tamed
dogs to help them track and
hunt for food. About eight
thousand years ago, ancient
Egyptians

raised **Saluki** hunting dogs.
Saluki is an **Arabic**
word meaning noble one.
These dogs are the oldest
known breed.

Although many <u>breeds</u> lay
claim to being the oldest, it is
probably the hound family
that can come closest to
this. Ancient Egyptians

domesticated dogs that are closely related to today's greyhound family (current breeds are the **Pharaoh, Saluki, Ibizan, Basenji** and Afghan). While the **Greyhound** may be the most elegant member of the hound family, today's family of hounds include such well known breeds as the Bloodhound, Beagles, Bassets and Dachshund among many others. Probably the first domesticated use of dogs, other than hunting, was for herding purposes.

Shepherds have used dogs
to
assist for millennia.

Eventually, man began to
realize dogs could be used to
perform other functions in
society. Selective breeding
was used to develop dogs
suitable to fulfill these
specific
tasks - guarding the village,
attack dogs during wars and
carrying or hauling goods
were
just a few examples.

 In relationship to their
size, dogs can haul

prodigious weights
as evidenced by
such breeds as
the American Eskimo dog.

Special dogs are trained
today for many tasks to
help humans. Guide dogs
help the blind, hearing aid
dogs, and dogs that work
with veterans. Many
functions have been found
that the dog can do to help
those with disabilities.

As the popularity of dogs
as companions developed
in the mid-19th century,
breeding

became more deliberate
with the idea to produce
breeds suitable to more
specific purposes.

The introduction of breed
or <u>kennel</u>
<u>clubs</u> encouraged not only
the introduction
of the "pet", they were also
primarily responsible for
the growth in breeds
today
considered show
dogs. <u>Kennel</u>
<u>clubs</u> introduced
accepted <u>breed</u>
<u>specific</u> traits
and introduced the idea of

groups of dogs, such as
sporting group, toy group
and working dogs.

Working Dogs

The Cat

Kitty loves to play and take
naps all day.

Kitty likes to meow and
watch the house.

Kitty never minds what
happens in her realm.

She simply is happy when
she is well fed and warm.

She loves to have
someone care for her and
gently stroke her back.

Kitty loves to play and take
naps all day.

The House Cat

The cat has been with us
for centuries often
worshiped and always
protected.

The favorite pet for little
girls and women. Many
men like to have her
around as well.

It is said that the cat is the protector that keeps the mice away. Today the cat is considered one of the world's most popular pets. The cat is domesticated and fits right into families with ease.

The beautiful cat is enigmatic very easy to care for and friendly. The cat has been with us for over 4,000 years. It is known that the Egyptians was the first civilization to use the cat to destroy any vermin.

In this manner the cat was able to help keep the food safe for eating. The cat was protected under their law if you harmed the cat you had to face the death penalty.

Cat Facts

- It has been scientifically proven that owning cats is good for our health and can decrease the occurrence of high blood pressure and other illnesses.

- Stroking a cat can help to relieve stress, and the feel of a purring cat on your lap conveys a strong sense of security and comfort.
- The ancient Egyptians were the first civilization to realize the cat's potential as a vermin hunter and tamed cats to protect the corn supplies on which their lives depended.

- Sir Isaac Newton is not only credited with the laws of gravity but is also credited with inventing the cat flap.
- A cat has more bones than a human being; humans have 206 and the cat has 230 bones.
- A cat's hearing is much more sensitive than humans and dogs.
- The cat's tail is used to maintain balance.

- Cats see six times better in the dark and at night than humans.
- Cats eat grass to aid
  their <u>digestion</u> and to help them get rid of any fur in their stomachs.
- A healthy cat has a temperature between 38 and 39 degrees Celsius.
- Cats have the largest eyes of any mammal.
- The female cat reaches sexual maturity at around 6

to 10 months and the male cat between 9 and 12 months.
- A female cat will be pregnant for approximately 9 weeks or between 62 and 65 days from conception to delivery.
- The average litter of kittens is between 2 - 6 kittens.
- Ailurophile is the word cat lovers are officially called.
- Purring does not always indicate that a cat is happy. Cats

will also purr loudly when they are distressed or in pain.

- All cats need taurine in their diet to avoid blindness. Cats must also have fat in their <u>diet</u> as they are unable to produce it on their own.
- In households in the UK and USA, there are more cats kept as pets than dogs. At least 35% of households with

cats have 2 or more cats.
- When a cat rubs up against you, the cat is marking you with its scent claiming ownership.
- About 37% of American homes today have at least 1 cat.
- Milk can give some cats diarrhea.
- The average lifespan of an outdoor-only cat is about 3 to 5 years while an indoor-only cat can live 16

years or much longer.

- On average, a cat will sleep for 16 hours a day.
- A domestic cat can run at speeds of 30 mph.
- The life expectancy of cats has nearly doubled over the last fifty years.
- Blue-eyed, white cats are often prone to <u>deafness</u>.
- The cat's front paw has 5 toes and the back paws have 4. Cats born with 6 or 7 front toes and

extra back toes are
called polydactyl.
- An adult cat has 30
teeth, 16 on the top
and 14 on the
bottom.
- There are
approximately
60,000 hairs per
square inch on the
back of a cat and
about 120,000 per
square inch on its
underside.
- Cats and kittens
should be acquired
in pairs whenever
possible as cat
families interact
best in pairs.

- In multi-cat households, cats of the opposite sex usually get along better.

Baby Kittens

The Elephant

The elephant is loved by all
He maybe big and strong
But he comes when you call
His trunk he uses to bath
His feet to stomp about
His ears flap in and out
As he is laughing when he walks
down the path
The elephant is friendly sort
With his tusk he is so proud
And his horn he blows to shout it
out

The elephant today is
faced with loss of habitat
and hunters who destroy
them for their tusk.

The place where they live
is becoming so much
hotter making it difficult for
them to forage for food.
The poor little calf has a
hard time surviving.

This can lead to the
destruction of the
elephants. The fact is that
poaching for the ivory
tusks has created the loss
of whole elephant herds.

We need to protect the elephant as they are a beautiful species.

Elephant Legends

1. The boy with the elephant head

One of the most well-known elephants in religion is the Hindu god Ganesh, who is depicted as a human with an elephant's head. One

Hindu story describes how
Ganesh was created by
the goddess Parvati, who
wanted a loyal son.
Parvati's husband, the
powerful god Shiva, had
been travelling while this
happened. He was startled
by young boy standing
near his home, so drew
his sword and severed the
child's head. Parvati was
enraged, and Shiva was

distraught. He sent his
soldiers out to bring him
the head of the first living
creature they came
across, which just so
happened to be an
elephant. Shiva attached
the elephant's head on to
Ganesh's body and
breathed life into it. He
then accepted the boy-
elephant hybrid as his own
son.

2. The white elephant with six tusks

Buddha is said to have incarnated as a white elephant several times. He once lived as Chaddanta, a white elephant with a scarlet face and feet and six tusks. He lived in a golden cave with two

wives, Mahasubhadda and
Chullasubhadda.
According to one version
of the Buddhist story,
Chaddanta insulted
Chullasubhadda by giving
his second wife a lotus
flower. Chullasubhadda
left him, and eventually
hatched a plan – with her
new lover the king of
Benares - to steal his
tusks as an act of

vengeance. The king
assigned a hunter,
disguised as a monk, to
retrieve his tusks.
Although the elephant
could have easily killed the
hunter, he recoiled out of
respect for religion. The
hunter eventually
explained the entire story,
and Chaddanta cut off his
own tusks, handed them to
the hunter and died. When

the hunter presented them
to Chullasubhadda, she
died of shock. Essentially,
revenge is no good.

3. The blind men and the elephant

This ancient Indian
parable tells the story of
six blind men who
encountered an elephant

for the first time. When
they set their hands upon
it, each blind man felt a
different part of its body –
its flank, its tusk, its tail, its
trunk, its ear and its leg.
The men all described
what they thought the
elephant looked like to
each other – one
described it as a mud wall,
one a spear, one a rope,
one a snake, one a fan,

and one a palm tree. They inevitably returned from their trip bickering about what the elephant looked like. This tale describes how essential it is to consider all views to build an accurate picture of reality: although all the blind men were partially right, they were all ultimately wrong.

4. The elephant and thunder

This Kenyan myth tells
how humans destroyed
the harmony of creation.
Three beings – the
elephant, man and thunder
– lived on earth, but didn't
get on because of their
vast differences.
Gradually, thunder
became afraid of man's
power and left earth for the

sky, whereas the elephant
stayed because he
thought man was small
and harmless.

When man and the
elephant were alone, he
fashioned poisonous
arrows and shot the beast
in the back. As the
elephant lay dying, it
wailed at the sky, begging
thunder to save him. But
thunder refused, saying

that the elephant's naivety
had killed him. As the
elephant died, man made
more poisonous arrows
and went on to kill more
living creatures, eventually
becoming the master of
nature.

ELEPHANT

The Dove

God appeared to us in the
form of a Dove, saying this
is my beloved son.

The Dove is beautiful in all
its splendor show its wings
unfurled and says well

done. The Dove is beauty
untold but the Love it gives
is easily shown.

We often find that we are
weak but in God his love
we seek. The Dove is
there to show the way. It
stands for peace in its day.

Make sure that you too
carry the Dove in your
heart the bird of Love.

The Dove lives in the open
country, woodland areas
and some are tame and
can be kept in your home
in cages.

The Dove is a beautiful
bird indeed. It likes to feed
on grassland, backyards,
and roadside areas. You
can buy Dove food which
is seed for the house
bound Dove.

Doves like to eat seeds,
cultivated grains, and
peanuts. Enjoy watching
them and listening to their
cooing.

The dove will nest in
dense foliage on the
branch of an evergreen,
orchard tree, mesquite,
cottonwood, or vine. It is
also common for them to
nest on the ground.

Clutch Size:	2 eggs
Number of Broods:	1-6 broods
Egg Length:	1.0-1.2 in (2.6-3 cm)
Egg Width:	0.8-0.9 in (2.1-2.3 cm)
Incubation Period:	14 days

Nestling Period: 12-15 days

Egg Description: Unmarked, white.

Condition at   Helpless, eyes closed, sparse
Hatching: hold up head, dependent on

The Dove is a special bird
with many people who love
to wear jewelry made of it's
symbol.

One of the most outstanding
birds well known and
recognized throughout the
world.

Two Doves holding wedding rings

ISBN 10: 1987617541
ISBN 13: 9781987617542